DAYS AND NIGHTS OF THE BLUE IGUANA

DAYS AND NIGHTS OF THE BLUE IGUANA

HEATHER ROYES

P E E P A L   T R E E

First published in Great Britain in 2005
Peepal Tree Press Ltd
17 King's Avenue
Leeds LS6 1QS
UK

ISBN 1 84523 019 1

 Peepal Tree gratefully acknowledges Arts Council support

CONTENTS

III SELECTIONS FROM 'THE CARIBBEAN RAJ'

I   DAYS AND NIGHTS OF THE BLUE IGUANA

DAYS AND NIGHTS OF THE BLUE IGUANA

One day when you and I
have gone our separate ways,
we will remember
the days and nights of the blue iguana.
And how the rain came down
at five in the morning
like white curtains of voile over the hills,
and how the red immortelle exploded in the valleys,
and how we laughed and laughed.

One day, when you and I
have unpacked in different cities,
and divided our books correctly,
we will remember how we drank coffee
on the verandah, and how
the blue iguana crept along the wall,
and stretching its long neck
performed its graceful toilette.
And how we laughed and laughed.

One day, when you and I
have gone our separate ways,
we will remember.

RETURNING TO HAVANA AFTER TWENTY FIVE YEARS

The rooftops of Havana called:
"Chica! What happened?
We thought you loved us – but 25 years?"
And the *Hotel Nacional*, refurbished, white
and gleaming in the sun – the Dowager! –
scoffed: "You said, 'I love you, Havana,
with your ice cream parlor lines...'
and you called me an ageing prostitute.
You've been to other cities,
you've had other loves."

Dazed by the immediate reconnection,
I mumbled: "It's a long story –
my life is complicated.
I wanted to remember you with dance and song –
not sorrow;
not bits-and-pieces clothing,
bad teeth and peroxide hair.
I never knew you'd wait."

The gargoyles on the Museo cackled:
"What an excuse! But here you are
and we're even better than before,
more faithful. We've never changed.
The tourists love us
and we go with them for money – not for love.
That we keep for you, who knew us,
in good times and in bad..."

Old Havana, beautiful, tattered,
languishing in the sun,
and the Malecon against the sea,
stretched and laughed, elasticising their images:
"We cling to you, like an old woman's girdle!"

Night comes in and with it – the camelo,
a dim orange world of reality, heaves up and down,
while hiding in the shadows,
the chiquitas, demure,
well dressed and registered at the nearby clinic,
await their clients for the night.

PARAMARIBO

Yellow flowers
shower the decaying wooden palace
lending an air of rebirth to Paramaribo
with its zangvogels in cages – everywhere,
and its pock-marked, shot-marked brick buildings,
exuding a glorious past before the coups.

The zangvogels,
small brown birds in their cages,
sing each Sunday morning in the market,
and the war-scarred city awaits recuperation.
Ghosts haunt the red-brick buildings
of Fort Zeelandia,
where old photos of the resplendent kottomissi ladies hang,
and black boys, stoked up on crack,
drive fancy cars through the swampy slums of Latour.

The flat, brown river stretches,
penetrates the Amazon,
giving promise of a more authentic life.
Trembling on the brink,
Suriname waits.

POSTCARD FROM THE WEST INDIES (CIRCA 1933)

Dear Beryl,

In some islands,
the boys dive for coins
tossed by tourists from the steamers,
their sleek, black bodies slicing the water.
What smiles, what guiles!
What fools are we!
Wish you were here.

BABYLON BE STILL!

In a small corner of the Western world,
where light reflects through banana leaves,
sitting on a verandah covered with vines,
I think of the significance of a Royal Death.
Hunted by the hounds of paparazzi,
adored, she revealed the fragile face of monarchy.

The agouti runs down a samaan tree
and wild kiskedees call.
A Rastafarian, bicycling through St. Ann's,
shouts: "Babylon! Be still!"

GUYANA SEAWALL

Looking out over the seawall,
I absorb the huge expanse, the frontierland –
and absolve my white ancestors.
I forgive all hurts and grievances
and lay to rest the relicts of my injury.

My grandfather, fiery, robust,
Sephardic, galloping across his estate,
impregnating mulatto women
from Phillipsburgh to Marigot
as well as his own wife
(thirteen – the lucky number!).

My grandmother, at eight years,
in bonnet, prim, high-topped, laced boots
and stockings, clinging
to the rails of a schooner
from Demerara to Port of Spain in 1903.
Tight-lipped,
she remembered the riots, the fire,
the death of her parents; and her sister, last seen,
running across the roof, nightdress ablaze.

What lives they led,
wandering up and down the islands.
What legacies they left, nomadic,
hot tempered, passionate in the belief
of their indistinguishable tribe.

THIS CREOLE VERSE OF DÉJÀ VU

Sitting among these paintings,
jungle colours of greens and blues,
flora and fauna of the Caribbean,
listening to Sodade music from Cabo Verde,
lusophonic boleros and meringues
("The Sea is the Home of Nostalgia..."
sings Caesaria Evoria).

Swaying rhythms,
tinny pianos and *fin de siècle* violins,
for twirling skirts
and sloping lawns. Transposed
into the hand-tinted evening light,
the smell of cut grass, bougainvillaea
arching everywhere and
white benches waiting.

Somewhere, you stand, across the years,
smiling in white apron, cap in hand,
Nanny, who held me close.

THE RED AND GOLD SWEET DREAMS SACHET

A wind-swept white apartment
overlooking the savannah and
Tranquility tennis courts.
Dry leaves swirl in the living room,
tuna for lunch
– there's nothing else.

No sign of struggle:
the bed, half made-up,
reflects no act of disenfranchisement,
no moments that will change your life
forever.
The Red and Gold Sweet Dreams sachet
lies undisturbed beside the pillow,
silent witness to your secret trauma.

The police had carefully
washed the glasses and,
turned them down to dry.
Your time had not come, though violated,
your card was not called.
Your life must spin out more Play Whe numbers,
and your dream-filled nights
their signs and symbols.

NO EXILE – SMALL SABBATICALS NOW AND THEN

No exile – small sabbaticals now and then.
But I could not leave the Caribbean –
always seeking the imbroglio of cultures,
constantly exhausted by my affairs.

But there were times in my life
when I languished like a Greek wife,
waiting for the Thesmophoria,
anticipating the exotic smell of burnt bulls,
the shattering of pottery and figurines,
curse tablets (naming names) half-buried in the sand.

Sometimes I yearned for cheap thrills –
the bellow of sacrificial animals,
the thud, the smell of blood.
Escaping to a pagan past,
I offered wild orchids to the Keeper of Fertility,
my Tenth Muse.

Resuscitated,
I returned to a greater god,
a blue icon, a childhood by the sea,
the greens and yellows of ocean floors –
swirled and circled by tropic storms and currents,
in peaks and troughs.
The boom sound of oars,
the swish of nets,
the slush-slush of waves on a quiet shore.

TRYING TO TRANSCEND THIS CARNAL CARTAGENA

Imprisoned in green cartwheels,
rainforest gardens
lush and weeping;
velour macaws in blue and orange,
toucans in red and black with hieroglyphic beaks
scream obscenely at the sky.

Stretched out
in an illuminated case,
clothed in empty bishop's vestments,
bones of the saint ("Slave of Slaves")
cast an eerie light
over the burnished pews.

An old mulatto woman,
kneeling in the back row,
head-tied and rosaried,
weeps for who-knows-what.
I genuflect, trying to transcend this Carnal Cartagena,
but still, you come to me in all your glory –
straining and impassioned.

A PLATE OF INCENSE

At midnight,
my daughter brings me
a plate of incense,
four sticks fluttering in the dark.
I grope for money,
shuffle and hurry back to sleep.

Small rituals for a New Year's Eve!
No parties, tuxedos,
dancing till four in the morning
as when, in a large convertible
I drove through sleepy streets,
following instructions
from my friend sprawled beside me,
much drunker than I thought.

Churchgoers and Revivalists,
returning home from 'jumping",
paused on the early morning sidewalk,
observing
the extravagant bourgeoisie.

THE MULATTRESS SAYS "IT HOT FI TRUE"

Rum-bellied, heavy breathing,
the Englishman (wig awry)
bent low on swollen knees to her.

Cleavage moist with sweat,
she closed her yellow eyes
and turned her head away,
choosing to regard a chocolate.
Blue taffeta crinkling
her cinnamon thighs,
she languished in the parlour –
fanning ("It hot fi true...").

All the field slaves, house slaves,
cooks, barrelwrights, clerks –
and tattered children too –
paid homage to her.
She knew her role,
she understood both sides –
where they met and where they came apart.

Ruminating slowly on a chocolate,
she smiled
and nodded an acknowledgement.

CAMPS-CAMPINS PAINTS A PURPLE EVENING AT DEVON HOUSE

A purple evening.
A few passé Creoles
in neutral colours,
and vivid throngs of dancehall donnettes,
their sons and daughters
and hairdressers – chemical duppies all –
with processed hair.
Red scallops and orange curlicues
pasted to their skulls.

Two cargo-chested Dons shocked out
in khaki colours,
protected by Dawg Heart cleaning his nails
with a ratchet knife.
Number Two, all perfumed and jerry-curled,
lounges in the foreground.

Thrown up by staged lights,
the bone-white mansion,
now a studio backdrop for slave weddings,
shudders through its Georgian facades
and colonnades. Flashing his gold tooth,
the Cotton Candy man smiles sweetly at my daughter:
"She's a regular," he says,
admitting me partly to the circle.

II WAJANG WOMAN

WAJANG WOMAN

Wajang woman,
you come like early morning storms
through Fondes Amandes.

I awake and feel you here,
jangling the verandah chimes,
rippling the venetian blinds,
puffing out the curtains.

You shudder and leave me
wondering how wonderful are early morning storms
through Fondes Amandes.

TO MY DAUGHTER – GABRIELA

I know that one day
you'll say "Moth-errr!
Did you have to write this?"
But I'll write it anyway.

Dear Gabriela, thank you
for saving my life, for lifting me up
when I was sinking. Thank you
for keeping me from becoming self-indulgent,
obsessed with small things –
my brush and comb laid neatly side by side,
my perfumes, medicines and personal
accoutrements laid out for finding in the dark.
My daily tasks shrunk down to petty rituals
of an insignificant survival.

As I review the blue toothpaste
remarkably drawn on the floor,
your yellow rubber duckies in the bath,
diapers in the wastebasket
and other signs of you scattered
throughout my life, I know that you
were after all what I'd been waiting for.

BUENA VISTA SOCIAL CLUB

The Chan Chan music of Cuba,
the little old men, smiling, smoking,
sitting with their legs crossed,
their guitars and their "son":
they remind me of my Makarenko Girl,
dancing, swaying,
singing the boleros
in order to survive the Revolution.

And how, in summer,
she ran in wooden flip-flop sandals from the bus,
(straw hat flopping, metal pail clacking)
to secure a hammock in the Special Country School
for sugar cane.
"You are a product of the Revolution..."
said the handsome young soldier,
smoking behind the barracks.
And how she marched proudly in khaki,
black shoes and brown beret for the Defensa Militar.

And then she began to run,
She was always running –
to see Alicia perform, to escape into a world of ballet.
Running to stand in line at Coppelia Ice Cream Parlour,
running to keep up with her husbands,
lovers, friends.
Running to become one of the privileged,
"on the official list for exotic orchids".

And then one day she ran away, escaping
from the world of special favours;
the neighbourhood committees,
the labs with their glistening pipettes
and translucent foetuses with curled fingers

like her unborn children;
the rations and the rumours,
the little old men with knowing smiles, singing
"The insane love of youth…"
Running, she has left me now,
marooned in cigar poster images,
listening to the Chan Chan music of Cuba.

YOU'RE STILL DANCING HORSEHEAD ON MY GRAVE

With tambourine and drum
you come, Set Girl,
ribbons flying, sashes flashing,
in blues and reds –
still dancing Horsehead on my grave.

Masquerading, fan-fana-ing.
Leaping, plunging, charading.
Jabbing flags,
tails, skins, bones,
and mirrors-mirrors-mirrors
catch the clamour of the crowd.

Children screaming,
boys shouting,
the Devil, red and horned,
prancing,
and you still dancing –
still dancing Horsehead on my grave.

LOVE IN THE MARKETPLACE

Sitting on my mother's verandah,
her spirit oozing through each chink and chad,
I put a name
to that feeling of rejection
which stays with you
forever...
after all these years
of seeking pain more real to me
than love itself which I had never known.

Love,
that came to me in the marketplace,
in a red turban,
green eyes and sandals too,
smiling, saying –
"I have come especially
for you."

CARNIVAL IN PORT OF SPAIN

J'ouvert Morning rising,
tearing through the streets,
ting-ting, ting—ing,
ping-ping-ping-ing through the black lanes.
Exploding into Monday Mas,
and with a pause, rocketing into Tuesday,
in orange, purple, blue sequins,
and pretty coloured girls with glistening thighs
and breasts too big for their costumes;
crazy, sunstruck tourists, drunk and dancing out-of-step,
one-two, one-two, down Tragerete Street.
All the time,
noise and screaming, whistles.

Shrieking outrageously across the savannah,
green parakeets with red-fringed wings
appalled by the invasion,
look for refuge from the noise.

We made love quietly in your house
surrounded by tall willows.
Outside, we could hear
"Down South! Down South! Down South!"

TABANKA, TARANGE AND FOOFOOROO

I know what you do,
don't think you can get away –
'cause I's keeping a file on you.
After all these years
and all the tears resolved,
I's laughing – *wha-a-a o-oh!*
Tabanka, tarange and foofooroo
'cause I's keeping a file on you.

YOU SEND ME A POSTCARD

After all these years
of hotel rooms and empty beds,
and things undone
and words unsaid,
I hear your voice and feel the same –
I cannot even call your name.

THE BOYS WE USED TO KNOW

Seagrape trees rub
their branches together,
squeaking and calling across the cliffs.
You lie beside me thinking of your affairs –
an unfinished painting beside you, mirroring
the sea and sky.

Shielding my eyes,
I drift away, wondering about life's patterns,
and why they are
how they are, cyclical,
unstoppable.

That evening, driving home
in the everafter rain of Junction Road,
we listen to Scoto "Il Castrata"
singing arias, and recall
the boys we used to know,
their arias and their anguish,
and how they passed away.

SOMEWHERE TODAY SOME MEN
WILL SPEAK OF POVERTY

Somewhere today,
thousands of crackling souls
waiting in dusty huts, will fade away.
Thousands more will look
for the last time
from their grimy cots
in hospitals that smell of urine,
with the huge, unblinking eyes of those about to die.

Somewhere today some men
will speak of poverty,
well-dressed in three-piece suits
counting their per diem at long polished tables
reflecting their exuberance.
Their oratory will excel, rise,
bounce off walls, rocket skywards
and spiral into the black holes of the universe.

ROMEO LAWRENCE GOES TO THE BARBER

Picking his way through the garbage,
Romeo Lawrence goes to the barber
on Upper King Street,
Hip-hopping like boys his age will do
on a Saturday morning,
dreaming of hairstyles
with shaved neckbacks and zigzag motifs and
Nike swooshes and "Badman" – though
he could not do it
because of school.

He sits in the barber's chair,
the white cloth wrapped around him,
listening to the chatter of the old men,
the gruff rough-and-tumble
that comes from old throats
the morning after white rum.
And the electric razor begins to buzz-zz.

Another noise takes over
from the doorway.
A youth, eyes afire,
pointing a trembling gun everywhere,
shouts, "Don't move!"
like in the movies and "Yu dead!"
Then Romeo Lawrence sees red
splish-splash drops on his white shroud
turning into rivers,
and his mind darkens
and his sneakers, stretched out before him,
covered in blood, fading away.

SAILING HOME FROM CHACACHACARE

Sailing home in the blustering afternoon,
we had to tack to-and-fro
through the straits
in the small red sailboat
named *Rogue*, leaning sideways,
lunging up and down.

By Gasparilla Grande,
a school of friendly porpoise
followed us in, jubilantly
jumping across the bow.
Two faithfuls stayed with us,
paralleling each other
in graceful, arching dives –
grey and white and slippery.

Sailing home from Chacachacare
the afternoon all blue and healthy,
we bade old ghosts goodbye,
leaving them floating
over the dry, rustling hills, the deserted
monastic houses, the derelict roads
– old ghosts singing "Ave Maria".

THE DRAGON SLEEPS TONIGHT

Sleeping among your things tonight –
your clothes, your time,
your space
gives me no thrill,
no grab-bag joy,
no hullabaloo like it used to.

Now it's just someone else's room –
the fan rotating quietly,
the elliptical mirror
winking at me in the dark.
In your small room the blinds drawn tight,
the dragon sleeps tonight.

III   SELECTIONS FROM THE CARIBBEAN RAJ

THEOPHILUS JONES WALKS NAKED DOWN KING STREET

On Monday, October 18th,
Theophilus Jones took off
his asphalt-black, rag-tag pants
and walked naked down King Street.
It was a holiday –
and only a few people saw
his triumphant march,
his muscular, bearded-brown body,
his genitals flapping in front.
Theophilus Jones had wanted
to do this for a long time.

At Towner and King, three carwash boys
shouting "Madman!" followed him to Harbour Street,
but seeing his indifference, turned
and dribbled back up the road.
Down on the Ferry Pier, a handful of people
waiting for the boat, stared out to sea
but did not see
Theophilus enter the water.

He walked out as far as possible,
then began to swim, strongly and calmly,
into the middle of the harbour.
Eventually, way out in the deep,
he stopped,
floated for a while, enjoying the sun,
watched a plane take off from the green-rimmed
palisades,
and then, letting himself go,
allowed the water
to swallow him up.

Theophilus Jones went down
slowly,
slowly his bent legs, slowly
his arms above his head,
slowly his locksed hair,
slowly.

Until nothing could be seen of him.
Some orange peel, an old tin-can
and a sea-saturated cigarette box
floated over his demise,
while nearby,
a kingfisher – scavenging for sprats
on a low current – veered down
and landed,
in a spray of sunlit water.

DEATH CAME TO SEE ME IN HOT-PINK PANTS

Last night, I dreamt
that Death came to see me
in hot-pink pants
and matching waistcoat too.
He was a beautiful black saga boy.
Forcing open the small door of my wooden cage,
he filled my frame of vision
with a broad white smile,
and as he reached for my throat,
the pink sequins on his shoulders
winked at me.

Last night, I dreamt
that Death came to see me in hot-pink pants.
He was a beautiful black saga boy
and I hit him with a polished staff
of yellow wood,
and he went down.
But as he reached for me once more,
laughing, laughing that saga-boy laugh,
I awoke, holding myself,
unable to breathe.
How beautiful was Death
in hot-pink pants with matching waistcoat too.

FOR A JAMAICAN SOLDIER KILLED IN VIETNAM

On the frontiers near Da Nang,
the wet and dirt, bellyache of fear and hunger
always with you, till when the fungus
on your feet, you too tired to scrape it off.
The rass rifle and sleeping bag,
extensions of your back,
become a part of you.
"Get your shit together and kill
those yellow motherfuckers,"
ambitious black sergeant tells you,
thinking he's going someplace 'cause
he thinks his race is going noplace.

Sometimes, just before shooting,
you see a face like Mr. Chin
who used to keep shop in Frankfield, Westmoreland,
or one of his sons who used to play with you,
and for an instant, you hesitate.
You see their faces
when they're about to die or already dead.
Eyes and mouths make frightened o's,
small limbs jerk, knees and elbows
in disjointed points
shudder at the sky.

Today, a bottleneck enclosed
by small yellow men in trees,
who you cannot see but know are there.
In the front, on the narrow jungle path
you run forward.
You run forward 'cause you sick and tired
of waiting,
and you sick and tired of the whole goddam war
which not fun anymore.

'Cause you seen too much blood,
and cause you want to tell them
to get out of your rass way,
so's you can get back to
Frankfield, Westmoreland.
Is no fun anymore this war.
Out of the bamboo,
which look just like the bamboo in St. Ann,
comes something small and hard
that hit you in the stomach.

Holding on, Lord, you holding on.
And the sky look blue above the bamboo
which is just like the bamboo in St. Ann,
and you on your knees, holding on.
The others running past, squish mud
into your face and eyes
wide – waiting for the pain to stop,
waiting in disbelief 'cause heroes
in the pictures never die.
And you see Westmoreland drifting by ...
small, dark room behind the shop,
the river and the faces saying,
"We waiting for you to come back!"
"I coming back. I's trying to come back!"
So you fall into the mud, and dirty boots,
going past you, running, say,
"Goodbye, son,
sorry 'bout Westmoreland, but we got to keep
pressing on."

XAYMACA, IS WHAT DO YOU?

Xaymaca, is what do you?
I love you so till,
I want to press myself
against your mountains and your seas
and make love to you.

Xaymaca, is what do you?
I want to kneel down
in front of you and worship you.
But you tear yourself
and your blood drenches my face
and fills my mouth
and suffocates me.

Xaymaca, is what do you?
I will give up all others for you
and I will be more faithful
than I have ever been before.
But you lie down with everyone,
and you fornicate with guns.

Getting down,
you look up at me
with your beaten-copper
slave collar,
and you laugh and laugh
and your scorn fills my ears,
and you betray me at every turn.

Xaymaca, is what do you?
I love you so till.

SINGING IN THE BATH WITH YOUR YOUNG SON

You
singing in the bath
with your young son.
Me
two walls away,
watching tv, wondering
how you look,
naked, shining-nude,
sloshing water.
But I can only hear you,
singing in the bath with your young son.

KENNEDY AIRPORT

Sitting in foreign airports
I dream of
things familiar,
familiar places,
familiar smiles, familiar thighs,
and remind myself
that
somewhere there is you.

Sounds come to me
filtering through my thoughts.
Faces pass as I sit waiting.

These strangers do not know you
but through me
they see you drifting.

TAKE TIME AND HEARTEASE WILL COME

This is the season of death –
but take time and Heartease will come.
As surely as the brown, testicular pods
come to the stinking-toe tree
in the Savannah,
and phoulourie ball sellers
throw out their smelly tents at night,
and as Lion Ice Cold Jelly Coconut van
parks lopsided on Maraval.

Take time and Heartease will come,
as yellow poui comes to the Liguanea Plains
before afternoon rains,
and red poincianas decorate the Mona Dam.
And as the John Crows land clattering
on hot tin roofs in summer,
mincing across pimento barbecues.

Do not rush to it,
but linger
like a virgin bride removing her white veil.
Savour grief and mourning with respect,
for they too, have their place.
Take time and Heartease will come.

I NO LONGER READ POETRY

I no longer read poetry.
I read obituaries,
horoscopes,
the classified ads, telephone directories
and notes to myself.

I no longer read poetry.
The images of Neruda,
Lao Tzu, Walcott and Senior
are curling,
yellow photographs, vaselined vignettes,
sepia scenes frozen in my memory.

I no longer read poetry.
I read Carl Stone's polls,
political speeches, Letters-to-the-Editor,
volumes of technical reports.
Even the *New York Times*
is a flight of fancy.

Mesmerised by the present,
forsaking the past, my mind,
a jealous lover, holds each moment
much longer than it lasts.
Time slips away and with it
dreams.
I no longer read poetry.

HALCYON DAYS IN CAPTAIN MORGAN'S NIGHTCLUB

Today, after fifty years,
I finally left my mother behind.
Sitting in Captain Morgan's Nightclub
in 1947, she was wearing
a fuchsia-red, long-sleeved blouse,
her dark hair swept back,
smiling her movie-star smile.
My father, elegant, urbane,
in a white dinner jacket.
Benevolent consort – distant prince.

Caught in time, they embellish
an old photograph, with other couples,
who – either too old, too drunk or
laughing too hard, peep sideways
at the charmed couple.
The two stare out kindly
at the camera, bemused by the attention.

Photo spots of brown and white
have corroded this halcyon image
that I have kept too lovingly,
too long.
Today, after fifty years,
I finally left my mother behind.

I WANT TO WRITE LIKE PABLO NERUDA

I want to write like Pablo Neruda
of pink clouds over Tegucigalpa
and poincianas fading into the hills,
of the wind howling
through Macchu Picchu.

I want to write like a *vaca sagrada*
in dark, baggy pants
of the *Violencia*, the wars
and the women.
But most of all,
of the moribund, grey mornings after.

I want to write like Gabriel Garcia Marquez
of topaz afternoons in Cartagena
and days turned to honey in Honda;
the decaying gentry, the mulattoes
and the madness, and always,
the oyster salt-smell of the sea.

Ojala —   to connect to Latin America —
to Bolivar, Maceo and Guillen,
to "Lucia, Lucia", and Marti,
to Sandra Cisneros, Javier Solis
and Xemanji.
If they will let me, I want to join
the great Carnaval of Life.

IN THE MIDDLE OF THE JOURNEY OF MY LIFE

In the middle of the journey of my life,
we surveyed Saigon,
picking through
the bric-a-brac of past lives,
in antique shops behind Tu Do.
Military medals, rusty G.I. tags,
Chinese opium pipes,
laid out like corpses
in long narrow trays.

In the middle of the journey of my life,
speeding through Hue,
we saw
schoolgirls bicycling in two's,
their white *ao dais* and long black hair
floating behind them.
Faces hidden in conic hats,
they remained concealed.

In the middle of the journey of my life
exhausted, I lay cold
in a hotel in Vung Tao
which used to be Cap St. Jacques.
The masseuse, young and warm,
placed my frozen hand between her thighs.
In the middle of the journey of my life.

HOTEL IN HAVANA

At four in the morning,
the busboys danced a flamenco
on the patio in the dark.
Looking down from the window,
I could not see them through
the thick, night-blackened palms,
but the rhythm of their heels and hands
staccato-ed up to me.

Sun-strobes began to light Havana Harbour,
throwing up rays behind Morro Castle,
sending stripes streaking
across the flat water,
and brightening the wide empty boulevards.

The hotel sat, with peeling facades,
like an aging prostitute
reflecting days of decadence
before the Revolution.
Decadence haunted the high ceilings,
swung from the chandeliers
and sent ghostly laughter
whirling down the long corridors.

I love you, Havana,
with your ice cream parlour lines
in 1950's fashions.
I love your bony, bare streets,
cleansed of urban crowds
rushing nowhere to do nothing.
Your once elegant mansions
now festooned with lines of washing,
your children with tomorrow faces,
your people and your austere dignity.

Sweet black coffee and harsh cigarettes
beside the pool where once
fat, white tourists bathed.
Workers on holiday vouchers
with un-hotel-like faces
wandering through the lobby.
The girl with the red *Defensa Militar*
armband who wore dangling earrings,
stockings, high-heeled shoes,
and chatted with her friend
behind the cigarette counter.

Later, in the evening,
two sharks swam lazily in the harbour,
while downstairs in the cabaret,
the rhumba dancer,
left over from other days,
shook out his equally ancient
black costume and prepared
his strands of hair.
There will be cassava and rice
on the menu again tonight.

SAMBA ON THE RADIO

If I were to write a poem this morning,
it would be about
samba,
Brazilian samba on the radio,
and afternoons on the patio overlooking sunsets
and parties and laughter.

This is to tell you how much you mean to me.
After all the nights of
pent-up feelings and talk,
(and how we talked!)
through telephone wires
crisscrossing the world
and cables under the sea.
How we consummated our love with words,
metaphors, literature, politics
and history.

If I were to write a poem this morning,
it would be about those times,
but most of all, about Brazilian samba on the radio.

GLOSSARY

p11: the *camelo* – El Camelo, the Cuban bus

p. 12: *zangvogels* – small birds of the lark family
kottomissi ladies – women in traditional Creole dress

p. 17: *Play Whe* – Whe-whe, a lottery based on 36 symbols, of Chinese origin.

p. 18: *Thesmophoria* – a women's festival, celebrated in Autumn, whose chief function was to promote the fertility of corn. It involved the sacrifice of pigs, hurled down into subterranean caves.

p. 25: *Wajang Woman* – loose woman or virago. (Trinidad)

p. 27: *Makarenko girl* – from the Makarenko Pedagogical Institute, named after Anton Makarenko, a noted Soviet pioneer of child development.
Chan-Chan – from the classic "son" of Compay Segundo.

p. 29: *Set Girl* and *Horsehead* – characters in the Jamaican Jonkunnu Festival which originated form slaves celebrating The New Year.

p. 31: *J'ouvert Morning* – the first morning of Trinidad carnival, traditionally marked by rough, mud-covered crowds, considered the authentic beginning of carnival from the 17th century.

p. 32: *Tabanka, Tarange, and Foofooroo* – an extreme form of Tabanka or love forlorn state (Trinidad).

p. 37: *Chacachacare* – and island south of Port of Spain, where nuns from the Dominican Order cared for lepers in the 19th and early 20th century.

ABOUT THE AUTHOR

Heather Royes works as a consultant in HIV/AIDS and as a poet, mainly in the Caribbean. She has been publishing since the 1970s and acknowledges the encouragement of the late John Figueroa, Mervyn Morris, Ken Ramchand and Ralph Thompson.

Prizes have included Silver and Bronze medals in the Jamaica Festival Literary Competition and the 1993 National Book Development Council Literary Competition. Her poems have appeared in such anthologies as the *Heinemann Book of Caribbean Poetry*, the *Penguin Book of Caribbean Verse* and the *Oxford Book of Caribbean Verse*. Her first collection, *The Caribbean Raj*, was published by Ian Randle Publishers in 1996.

Heather Royes was educated in Jamaica and the United States, and has travelled widely in her work as a consultant. She writes: "This type of travel has been my education as a writer and poet. When I experience cultures which are so far from mine, it gives me a feeling of learning just a little bit more about life and people."

OTHER JAMAICAN POETRY TITLES FROM PEEPAL TREE

Opal Palmer Adisa, *Caribbean Passion*
1-900715-92-9 £7.99

Lloyd Brown, *Duppies*
0-948833-83-1, £6.95

Kwame Dawes, *Progeny of Air*
0-948833-68-8, £7.95

Kwame Dawes, *Prophets*
0-948833-85-8, £7.95

Kwame Dawes, *Jacko Jacobus*
0-948833-85-8, £7.95

Kwame Dawes, *Requiem*
0-948833-85-8, £5.99

Kwame Dawes, *Shook Foil*
1-900715-14-7, £7.99

Kwame Dawes, *New and Selected Poems*
1-900715-70-8, £9.99

Marcia Douglas, *Electricity Comes to Cocoa Bottom*
1-900715-28-7, £6.99

Gloria Escoffery, *Mother Jackson Murders the Moon*
1-900715-24-4, £6.99

John Figueroa, *The Chase*
0-948833-52-1 £8.95

Delores Gauntlett, *The Watertank Revisited*
0-84523-009-4

Jean Goulbourne, *Woman Song*
1-900715-57-0, £6.99

Rachel Manley, *A Light Left On*
0-948833-55-6, £5.99

Earl McKenzie, *Against Linearity*
0-948833-85-8, £7.95

Earl McKenzie, *The Almond Leaf* (forthcoming)
1-84523-012-4, £7.99

Anthony McNeill, *Chinese Lanterns from the Blue Child*
1-900715-18-X, £6.99

Geoffrey Philp, *Florida Bound*
0-948833-82-3, £5.95

Geoffrey Philp, *Hurricane Center*
1-900715-23-6, £6.99

Geoffrey Philp, *Xango Music*
1-900715-46-5, £6.99

Velma Pollard, *Crown Point*
0-948833-24-6, £7.99

Velma Pollard, *Shame Trees Don't Grow Here*
0-948833-48-3, £6.99

Velma Pollard, *Leaving Traces* (forthcoming)
1-84523-021-3, £7.99

Ralph Thompson, *The Denting of a Wave*
0-948833-62-9, £6.95

Ralph Thompson, *Moving On*
1-900715-17-1, £7.99

Ralph Thompson, *View from Mount Diablo*
1-900715-81-3, £7.99

Gwyneth Barber Wood, *The Garden of Forgetting*
1-84523-007-8, £7.99

All available from Peepal Tree Press's website, with secure, on-line
ordering. Visit peepaltreepress.com
or contact us my mail at 17 King's Avenue, Leeds LS6 1QS, UK